The Journey Shall Go On

AuthorHouse™
1663 Liberty Drive
Bloomington, IN 47403
www.authorhouse.com
Phone: 833-262-8899

Because of the dynamic nature of the Internet, any web addresses or links contained in this book may have changed since publication and may no longer be valid. The views expressed in this work are solely those of the author and do not necessarily reflect the views of the publisher, and the publisher hereby disclaims any responsibility for them.

Any people depicted in stock imagery provided by Getty Images are models, and such images are being used for illustrative purposes only.
Certain stock imagery © Getty Images.

This book is printed on acid-free paper.

ISBN: 978-1-6655-1649-5 (sc)
ISBN: 978-1-6655-1648-8 (e)

Library of Congress Control Number: 2021902947

Print information available on the last page.

Published by AuthorHouse 03/08/2021

authorHOUSE®

The Journey Shall Go On

DEBORAH PEGLER

Yellow rose-joy, gladness, delight, infection, friendship and caring and reassurance of a new beginning.

Table of Contents

To all the beautiful souls
that have touched my heart
along the way to my recovery.

For all the loses and the gains
that have made my life a journey,

and to God who lifts me up,
for to him I give all the glory.

I

Mother

I received the most beautiful gift from my child today,
helping me get in touch with my true self once again.
This I thank you for — thank you for teaching me faith,
trust in a higher power, and in myself.

For all emotions that are tense and strong,
and utmost knowledge I have lived for these.
Lived deep, and let the lesser things live long.
The everlasting hills, the lakes, the trees,
who'd give their thousand years to sing this song.

When I Feel Like Screaming

I'd rather scream it out on paper
than to let you see me cry.
The bottom line is trust,
but then that's the reason why?

So many people mistreat this
In our materialistic world.
Trade the value of a friendship
for the value of a pearl.

Along our journey to be one
we see many pains we have brought.
Realizing that so many times
our mistrust is why we fought.

It is something that only we can
change within ourselves as we
do see, and pray our friends can
do the same or we must set them free.

The decision to let go is a
painful one, but a healthy one at that.
For if someone in your life can be
so cold then their karma is where
it is at.

Maybe someday they will see the pain they put
on another's soul.
But until that day yes it is safe to say,
I can do better for I am whole.

A Safe Place

In the darkest of this new world
this new world we've come to know.
You gave me a safe place,
a place where I can go.

You opened up a door for me
my heart you've caused to smile.
Called me apart to a safe place,
so I could rest a while.

When you listen to my story
your love caresses me
to know that you are my comfort
a peace comes over me.

I trust you Lord with all my heart,
the bigger picture you do see,
the joy you bring into my heart
your arms will shelter me.

To know that you are near
tell me Lord who shall I fear
when the mountains are cast into the sea,
these things shall pass I do believe.

So I thank you for my safe place
a place where I can go.
To protect me from the dark side
in this world we've come to know.

The Missing Link

A free man he roams
this ground alone,
in search to join his companion.

With ease he treads,
as he prolongs his quest,
fearing most what he passionately dwells on.

In a haze he will find,
memories left behind,
and a picture of faded emotion.
As he secretly cries,
and the memory dies,
he moves on with a sense of devotion.

At the core of his heart,
digging deep, one more start,
to discover the link to his union.

Deep inside he will see,
and the answer will be,
satisfying the yearning to be one.

V

As we walk the walk

As we walk the walk with the Lord,
with belief of the promise land.
Like pillars we stand, one by one hand in hand,
Letting winds of heaven flow
between praying for wisdom, your way to be seen
as the time passes by like the wink of an eye
Trials and testings we all knew there will be.

Let us stick to the word, like we've so often heard
And our Lord be our counsellor, Pray Thee.
As we stand solid ground and his spirit will surround,
to protect us and guide us through and through.

Praise you Jesus! Give God the glory,
without faith, there is no story.
Givinjg thanks to the prayers we ask of you.
almighty one, you gave this union
something to cherish, how we are blesed
and we know you love us oh so Lord
For to us you manifest
and we pray we always reach out to you Lord
and we will truly give our best
step by step, day by day with our prayers
and you will do the rest.

Never Did He Leave

In the midst of all the madness the insanity we've come to know,

just stop wallowing in the sadness and start learning to let go.

Beyond the power of the mind games, and the fear of losing control,

the torment of the emotional tug-of-war that's only killing our souls.

Remember the road that awaits us isn't always what we would choose,

so we hang on in desperation cause we're so afraid we'll lose.

"If only this went my way, it would be easy, don't you see?"

But something much more powerful has a different plan for me.

Not always what I wanted, and sometimes brought great pain,

but never did he leave me, and when I lost,

I gained.

VII

Darkest Dream

She walks this plain in wonder of a future she cannot see.

Though guided by whats beyond her she strives to be set free.

She knows she has a purpose, but she craves the love she needs.

Still her inner child feels empty for it's her inner soul that bleeds.

When her feelings of unholiness leave her feeling she has sinned,

and wondering if there is a light, not sure of a place to begin.

There's a world she's vaguely familiar and a story to be told, one that's

deep, and dark, and fearful hanging desperately to her soul.

Going back she finds the answer within a shadow she's sometimes seen.

And together they find salvation in the distance of her darkest dream.

VIII

Reflections

Not even the rain can even wash away the pain now,
all the emotional sorrow gleaming through my teardrops
can splash a picture of the love I am holding on to.

Sadly I am walking away and letting go of the memory
this picture shows.

Hoping the sun will shine again and what tomorrow brings,
who knows.

IX

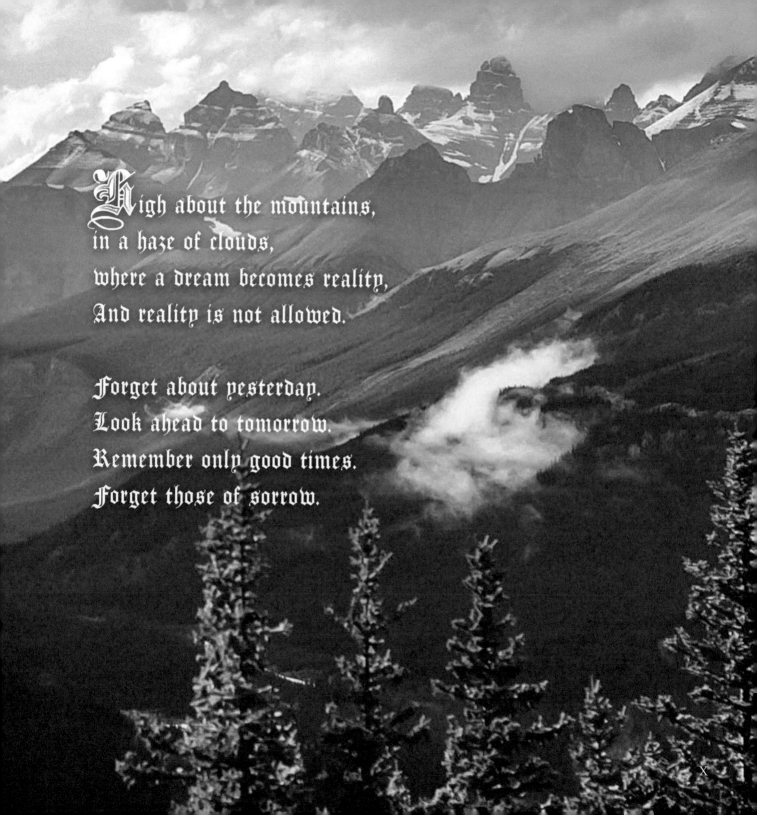

High about the mountains,
in a haze of clouds,
where a dream becomes reality,
And reality is not allowed.

Forget about yesterday.
Look ahead to tomorrow.
Remember only good times.
Forget those of sorrow.

X

Listen to the Laughter

Hear the laughter of the children, what sweet music it sings, to free us from the heartaches that life sometimes brings.

See the happiness and wonder they have on their face, while telling a secret, feel them touch us with grace.

What is their secret? Are they holding the key? Can their wisdom now help us with life's mystery?

Just a puzzle we're placing one piece at a time, even when we are brainstorming they have peace of mind.

So let us beware of the wisdom they have got, they are trying to teach us, life has no plot.

This spiritual freedom we cannot ignore, the magic is in their laughter, they have been here before.

Not Forever

Never did we say it would be
forever, but in our minds
we thought it could be

and how our hearts would break
when we said goodbye
cause the end was not for us
to see

If only we could love one another
as the last day we intended to see

Say a kind word and hug one another
no regrets will there ever have to be

Have faith when we part
separate lives, brand new
starts may not bring us all together
let us not take for granted
the special ones we love
may be chosen anytime
from above.

XII

If We Could Change The Mind of Fate!

Drawing you closer,
Through the window of my eye,
burning passion penetrates to the soul.

When you lock on so tight,
and you are wondering why,
yet you let down the walls built so tall.

When you know you are defying,
there is no meaning to the law,
and you know that you have past that fine line.

Still the feelings so strong,
you think you wanna cry,
then you try to run,
but you are mine.

Here I am I surround you,
I'm above you, all around you.
Umm! Can you feel the rythem within'!
Can you find a good reason to pursue nature's sin!
Or will you let fear itself suck you in?

When you pencil me in,
Will you do it in ink?
Give this story a chance to unveil.

Or can something so good,
Turn to something so bad.
Depressed, sad, and Angry,
Now the title of our tale.

Must the love fade away,
Like the words of a song.
Never knowing the pleasures
that might be.

If only we could read the mind of fate
Be content with the things that we see.

Would we make a turn
from that tunnel so deep?
Would there ever have been

You and me?

XIII

I wouldn't have it any other way!

You woke me up this morning,
put a song upon my heart.
Like a jay bird singing,
this was just another start.
to our time together
a start of a new day.
I wouldn't have it any other way.

Like a bubbling river,
the joy comes over me.
to know that you are with me
and there you'll always be.

You stick closer than a brother,
there is just no words to say,
I wouldn't have it any other way

I thank you lord for being here today, I
thank you lord for showing me the way
you give me strength to make it through
each day, you are in my heart and that is
where you are going to stay.

You woke me up this morning and
whispered in my ear, you gave me every
word I breathe, to my eyes you brought a
tear.

To know that I'm with my best friend
there is just no words to say, I wouldn't
have it any other way.

Fate

I feel like I have been beaten inside,
I feel like screaming at the world.
Why me?

I wonder why I have to feel this pain,
has my life all been in vein?
I wonder why me?

But then I think of the lessons I have learned,
and how I can relate.

And then I realize it is not me.
These things have happened by fate.

I know I have a ways to go
before I have learned it all.

But I must remember
the pasts' the past,
move on and let it go.

In memory of Shirley,
a kind and gentle soul.

Changes

Through each changing season as it passes through my head,

I feel the emotion, another ending, another start.

As I look around me, the breeze blowing through the trees.

The grass so green, the birds flying free.

It's so symbolic this life we share,

Like the world around us are the people who care .

In and out of our lives like the changing of time.

Touching each others hearts, nothing yours, nothing mine.

So as we look back a clear picture we'll see

When we let go of one yet another shall be

and to see straight a wise man you will me. for the future is only for the profound to see.   XVI

From Within

Let us start a little journey of the body, mind, and soul. Serenity and purity, the nature of our goal.

Going back to the beginning where life's healings so clean and pure, when nature was the only way, good health we did ensure.

Let us start our lettle journey, let us INTRA from within, just take the key to be set free and your story shall begin.

As we travel back together, telling tales of ecstacy, like on most exctiing journeys, little tests there are bound to be. Yet, we must not be discouraged, for this is nature at its best, have the power to go forward, it will naturally do the rest.

And as sure as nature's blossom, soon a flower you shall be, and with all the hope of yesterday, we'll live in harmony.

Not saying goodbye . . .

Sitting here looking
at the peace and tranquility
in your face as you sleep,

Wanting to caress you,
thou shall not weep.

Wanting to come over and hold you so,
afraid of the pain,
not wanting to let go.

And so I leave,
not saying goodbye,

though I'm breaking inside,
I will not deny.

This is just the beginning, not another end.

So I wish you well,
and take care,
my beautiful, beautiful friend.

Freedom

The peace and tranquility I get from the sea,

the feeling of freedom is sheer ecstacy.

the feeling to know that I am free,

the feeling to know I am free to be me.

Footsteps to Freedom

Admitted that I was powerless, with my life I've lost control. Reaching out for something to save and cleanse my soul. Although sometimes it is not easy, and not always could I submit, I decided to turn it over, and let the power deal with it.

I decided to look in the mirror as foggy as it may be, but I didn't see the reflection of the fear that's haunting me. Though soon I will come through it, and the good I'll see in me. I know I have a dark side, I admit this side I see, and I know with trust in the power, of these defects I'll be set free.

To all of you I have brought pain, I am willing to make amends, and hope for your forgiveness, I hope we'll remain friend. I promise to frind the courage, and admit when I am wrong. To believe in all my power from which I will grow strong. It's something that I've done before, a secret it's not to me. It's a story that's been told

My father called me loud and clear, but I just looked, turned my deaf ear.

I cannot go I'm not willing to say the things he wants I just walked away.

I carried on walking, thou I kept him in mind. I hid behind sin an easier way I shal find.

I would speak of a power in a round about way I didnt want others to see me that way.

I walked amongst thieves and drunkards for years i'd even submit to the bitter sweet tears.

I joined in the game, trying to be the same and all of the while, fathers calls out my name.

I weathered the storms feeling something with me i searched all the avenues but I still could not see.

I prayed for direction, I turned over my pain, started thinking more clearly, still im hearing my name.

I know god is calling, can't he see I lost my way, over again I turn it over, and I'm praying every day.

I'm told he has a humor, this I learned this special day. For when I finally heared his soft spoken word, wasn't he who had gone away.

Feeling safety in his presense this is it, I'm finally home, thank you father, please forgive me for so far

I had to roam not knowing what I was doing one more thing you wanted to say,

You say your name is Jesus, I believe you, please show me the way.

I look forward to our journey, thank you Jesus every day.

Please Don't Say Goodbye To Me

If the road we travel comes to a fork,
and we know it is meant to be
that we choose to walk a different path,
please don't say goodbye to me.

Let the winds of heaven
flow between us.
However far apart we may be
just remember I am with you
and you'll always be with me.

May the music trigger memories
feelings of gladness, sometimes sad,
and together in spiritual harmony
keep alive the time we had.

Thank yous

I would be honored to give a thank you and God bless to the many close friends and family that have helped to make my dream come true.

Writer and author: Debbie Petrie

Adam and Katie: for all the miles you have traveled and still come back to me.

Wayne: for being there at the right time, for getting me started again, giving me that little nudge.

Posers: Valerie Rose Beevor, Adam White and Katie, Tyler White, Jordan White, Debbie Petrie, Shirley pegler.

And last but not least the dream team of art, with all the spiritual energy, tone, rhythm and touch.

I thank my son Devon Petrie and our loving friend Ron Singh thank you so very much for making my dream come true.

Printed in the United States
by Baker & Taylor Publisher Services